CONFESSIONS OF A MELANATED

QUEEN:

Complexities of the Modern Black Woman

Dr. Lauren T. Meeks

DEDICATION

This book is dedicated to all melanated women who strive to do their life's work, with or without the validation of others. I am thankful that God has blessed me with the skills and ability to serve his people. I hope and pray that each of you find the strength and courage to follow your own path, build our own stage, and never wait for someone to give you what you deserve. YOU are responsible for making it happen.

INTRODUCTION

Confessions of a Melanated Queen was written to empower other melanated women who are interested in gaining support through stories, testimonies, and input from other women who look like them. Recently, I realized that I have a lot of opinions on topics that I never share with anyone. In the age of social media, it's quite easy to take a quick look at someone's life and assume they have it all together. Pride keeps us from sharing our truth. Instead, we take the best selfies (filtered and always angled to show our best side), show the attractive side of our relationships (nobody EVER makes a post after an argument). And we love to show off our kid's perfect report card (omitting the struggles leading up to those grades).

I'd like to take this time to confess. I confess that my way of thinking has not changed much over the years. However, I have made plans that didn't go the way I pictured them in my head. It's easy to say what we plan to do, but when your time comes, you may learn that your plan was not HIS. Or perhaps the results were not what you expected. Listen...that's ok. It's all about how you choose to move forward.

I hope you find this book helpful. The stories are raw but realistic. I want to thank the many women who participated in my online survey that I distributed while conducting research for this book. Your transparency is truly appreciated, and your words added the much-needed value to this project.

Best,

Dr. Lauren Meeks

TABLE OF CONTENTS

Confession One

I'm a Student of Everyone and Everything

I confess: I am a life-long learner. Not a life-long learner as in professional student, but a learner of life. There is no person too old or too young to teach me. I learn through mistakes, triumphs, trials, and tribulations.

Confessions of A Melanated Queen is a compilation of deep thoughts I currently have or held over the years that are rarely shared with others. What I learned through this process, and with the feedback of over 60 other Black women, is that we all have thoughts that we choose not to share. Sometimes it's because we don't want to be offensive, sometimes we prefer not to debate, and sometimes we realize that our opinion is just that, our opinion.

The beauty about sharing your opinion is that someone may be inspired by you. Also, by listening to others, you too may become inspired. Sometimes, there is no right or wrong answer, but a different perspective can change the way you look at a situation. That's why I find it so important to listen to others.

While writing this book, I had moments when I would get stuck and struggle to find the words to express how I feel. I put it down for a few days and go back to living. Without question, there was always a conversation, experience, or even something I witnessed that sparked my inspiration again.

I always tell people: I am a student of everyone and everything. I learn continuously. I'm inspired often. I am frequently enlightened. In this book, I discuss my thoughts on career upward mobility, marriage, parenting, the Black church, raising Black boys, feminism, and the perfect life. My inspirations from all these topics are derived from life experiences.

I encourage you to listen, to learn, and to never look down on someone because of their youth. Also, never ignore someone because of their maturity in age. There is wisdom at every stage.

In 2016, I founded We City, a nonprofit organization that aims to build communities through servant leadership. The truth is I started We City, NFP because I grew tired of having a lot of ideas, passions, and goals that were not met at my regular 9-5 job. I started a youth program, and I sold the idea to a few schools that expressed interest in picking it up. In that process, I learned that starting and operating a nonprofit is difficult. It's even tougher when you don't have the financial backing to support your efforts. I probably spent thousands of dollars over the past year launching, marketing, and sustaining my program. The question that I grapple with right now is: *is this project hurting or elevating my livelihood?* I have decided to scale back on the level of attention that I give to the program and focus on efforts that will generate revenue for my family.

I share this because the lesson I learned throughout this process is to take time to learn from yourself. I have learned to constantly evaluate my situation and determine if it is worth pursuing, warrants a break, or should be dismantled altogether. I choose to focus on *Confessions of a Melanated Queen*, which is my blog and now my first book.

This is what I do. This is my passion.

"*Being a Black woman, I feel that everything is a struggle. I think society has this perception that we are always strong and never have moments of vulnerability. In our careers and education, we are somewhat taught that we have to be two times better than our counterparts, and I think that is a major problem*" *Melanated Queen, 35 years old.*

Confession Two

Screw Your Corner Office

I confess: I don't want your corner office and I could care less about being somebody's boss. Now before you question my ambition, let me explain. Millennials have been characterized as self-absorbed, socially conscience do-gooders who are more interested in finding meaning in their work than making an extra dollar. We are less likely to retire before 70 and are more likely to live with our parents longer than our Generation X and Baby Boomer counterparts. I would agree that much of this is true. Black women, especially, have been raised to go to school, pursue advanced degrees, be independent, make moves, and be a boss.

The question I have is: *what does being a **boss** actually mean?* Traditionally, being a boss meant landing the perfect job, getting the promotion, and increasing your salary. For my generation, being a boss is much more than supervising others. It's your brand; it's supplemental income. It embodies autonomy, and it definitely does not include kissing someone's butt to make it. Being a traditional boss was never my goal. Besides, if I had never questioned my career goals, it was made clear four years ago.

The day was April 1, 2014. I was at my desk when I received an email from the person serving as the interim administrator over the department in which I worked. This was the job I planned to retire from, and I had grown very comfortable in my position. I dedicated my life to helping others, and in that role, I was able to do just that. The email indicated that we needed to go upstairs to the Vice President's office to discuss a meeting that was held earlier that day.

I arrived at that office to learn that I was brought to this meeting under a false pretense. This meeting had nothing to do with a follow-up. It was an ambush. I was questioned about some decisions I had made over the last three years while serving as the director of a program that was designed to graduate community college students on time and successfully transfer them to four-year institutions.

It was that moment that I realized that I had been deceived, lied to, and set up to be made an example of what not to do. You can't get away with empowering Black people without consequences. I found a way to help my students become successful and that included helping low-income community members avoid taking courses in which they would not earn college credits. Why? Because it was wrong to rob people of their time and money. My way of doing business did not profit the institution much, so I had to leave. By April 11th, I was escorted out of the building. By April 29th, the board voted to terminate my employment.

This experience is where my journey to finding *my* truth began. Up until this moment, my life had been perfectly planned out. I graduated from college on time, and I immediately enrolled in a graduate program. I completed that program within a year and began working at my dream job, where I was now being fired. I married at 25 and became a mother at 26. The only thing I had left to do in life was to continue to save for my retirement, plan vacations, be a good wife, and raise my son.

I soon discovered that for years I did a lot of things wrong. I had made the mistake of allowing my career, and specifically my employer, to serve as a major part of my identity. Now, that part of myself was gone, and I needed to figure out my next steps. To be honest, it took me years to get over it. That's because I never had a plan B, C, or D. I was foolish enough to put all my time and energy into one place and it nearly cost me my sanity.

Now, about that corner office…screw it. That same sentiment applies to the big dogs on the top floor who believe they have the power to make or break your career advancement. Screw them too. During my years studying sociology, I spent many days in the classroom discussing the notion that our careers define our master status. Even long before I got the boot, I decided that I would not allow myself to fight over positions that were more than likely pre-decided on by the powers that be.

I watched many Black female administrators work day and night to prove they were worthy of upward mobility within their organizations, only to be told "maybe next time", or "Sarah was just a better fit". I have personally been involved on both sides of the coin when upper management decided to pit one Black woman against another. And trust me, that sucked. Participating in the destruction of another Black woman brought so much guilt to my life, especially considering the fact that I have always been hired and mentored by Black women. Thank God that my involvement in such behavior was forgiven by the Sista' that I helped hurt. Yes, even I got caught up in the madness.

I witnessed Black women be used as puppets to keep others in line. I can recall reaching out to the woman who gave me my first job as an academic advisor. This was a woman I truly respected and felt forever indebted. Shortly after hiring me, she had lost the race for a cabinet position and moved on to another role at another institution. Several years after her departure, I was promoted to the position that I would later lose. I wanted her advice on leadership, and she encouraged me to return to school to earn my doctorate, but she also said something that I found interesting. She cautioned me to be mindful of our industry, and that there was a strategic effort to place Black women in highly stressful, middle management and administrative positions. These employers then pay you less than your White female and male counterparts, build a glass ceiling so that you can't climb further, and allow you to suffer from burnout before you are anywhere near retirement. Her advice was to pay attention to the positions that they "save for their children" and pursue those opportunities. I was stunned. Honestly, I didn't fully understand it, until I experienced it myself.

Don't think that I am against climbing the career ladder. I am all about Black women making money, enjoying life, and making moves. However, we should never place all our eggs into one basket, and we definitely need to stop letting others determine our worth. For those ladies who have worked hard to earn that corner office, I'm proud of you. Be sure to look out for yourself while you are in there. Also, whenever you can, reach back and pull another melanated Sista' or Brotha' up there with you.

To that end, the last four years have been interesting. I transitioned into the nonprofit sector. I enrolled in school and completed my doctorate degree. I founded my own nonprofit, and I discovered that I love research! These last four years taught me a few things: as previously discussed, never rely on one stream of income, never allow your current situation to define who you are, and never compromise your integrity, not even for your dream job.

I share this story because it marked the beginning of a new era for me. My termination forced me to work outside of my community. It was then that I began to learn more about the common struggles Black women face. Black women have been left with the responsibility of balancing their health, careers, intimacy or lack thereof, motherhood, friendships, and serving our community. Over 60 Black women completed a survey to provide data to support the themes of this book. One of the questions I asked the respondents was to share common issues that modern Black women face. A 34-year-old melanated queen spoke to this issue stating, "As black women, we're still trying to fit in and find our place in this white dominated world." Another participant, 34, shared her frustrations regarding barriers in achieving career advancement. She shared, "You are passed up for positions you're well qualified for because an older White person fears your education."

Here is the problem: as the women in the testimonies shared, it is extremely difficult for Black women to be their authentic selves. White privilege, White supremacy, and White feminism (yes, I said it), have served as barriers to our success. Nonetheless, what about the fact that often *we* are part of our own demise? A 40-year-old melanated Sista' shared the following:

"We need to start lifting each other up instead of tearing each other down. We are our own worst enemy. We talk about each other in [a] negative aspect and do not get why no one is surprised when we fail. If we expect better from each other, we must do better. We are not in this race to challenge each other, we are in it to support each other until we get to the finish line. Some lines may be closer than another person's line, but we need to support each person individually on their race. Stop the gossiping and the giddiness when you see a friend or coworker fail. Instead, pick them up and find out how you can potentially help them to finish their race."

This statement was powerful for several reasons. The person who sent me to the Vice President's office under false pretense was a Black woman. Jealously, backstabbing, hate, and the crabs in a barrel mentality is real. But why? Most of the time it's because of that damn corner office. Everyone wants it, so we, including Black women, are willing to do whatever it takes to get it, especially if another woman poses a threat to your plan to get there.

This Sista' continued with her statement regarding the Black woman's journey stating:

"If we are forced to run this [journey] on our own, with no one in our corner, it will become a harder struggle. And if we make it on our own, we become bitter people because we had to do this on our own. I strongly believe in lifting my African American women up. I will do everything I can to assist them along their journey. [It's] just sad that there are not too many people out there that believe in this."

She's right. We must do better. We must find other ways to define our success. Also, we must believe that the corner office, the big chair, the dope title, or any other symbol of being a boss, is not the be all, end all to your success.

I'm not against upward mobility. I don't think that it's wrong to desire leadership positions. I certainly do not believe women should stop aiming high in their respective careers. However, I do believe we need to define success differently.

Start a small business. Volunteer your time. Mentor girls and pour your knowledge into them. Write a book! Be a boss by your own standard. If it is going to compromise your personal values, don't even think about it! Build your own path!

Confession Three

I May Not Send My Kid to College

I confess: I have a doctorate degree, and I do not wish for my

son to follow in my footsteps. Don't get me wrong, higher

education is important. However, traditional and non-traditional

approaches to post-secondary education should be explored, and I'll

explain why. Most of my peers are proud holders of advanced

degrees they are still paying for. Most of us owe more in student

loans that we will ever make in an annual salary. In addition, you

have those who spent years and money on an education that they

will never use.

I was a first-generation college student. Neither one of my

parents completed a four-year degree, but they were very

supportive of my decision to attend a traditional four-year college. I

started off as a nursing major. Guess what? I didn't have a clue

about human anatomy and struggled all my life with math. I didn't take the right classes in high school to prepare me for the rigors of a health professions program.

After changing my major four times, I settled for a degree in sociology. I'm not suggesting that there is anything wrong with that, but had I been prepped for a nursing program in high school, I would have stuck with nursing. Nurses are always employed, although I do believe we have to get out of the habit of only teaching our kids about nursing. There are a lot of careers within the healthcare industry. Our youth need to know about the many other opportunities out there. Some examples are occupational therapy, speech and language pathology, audiology, physical therapy, and genetic counseling.

Now, back to sociology. After settling for a degree in sociology, I decided that I wanted to spend the rest of my life helping other young people successfully attend and graduate college. I sought out to be an academic advisor. I specifically wanted to work at a community college because I wanted to work with, well…the community. It was important for me to meet people where they are and help them build their dream career.

Here is my concern: thousands of parents are more focused on the idea of their children getting accepted to college than what they will do with their degree. Raise your hand if you know someone with a degree in history and working as a waiter. I do! No disrespect to them; an honest dollar is an honest dollar. However, one must question if they are truly getting a return on their investment. Parents should consider the following:

Trade/Vocational Programs

Have you ever seen a broke plumber? What about an unemployed electrician? Do you think mechanics sit around waiting for a job to call them? Unless they simply cannot do the work anymore, no one with a skilled trade goes hungry. When I was working at the community college, I saw some of the most amazing outcomes from our industrial trade programs. Some of the students who spent two years studying to be an electrician came out of school to job offers starting at $50,000 or more. Within a few years, those same associate degree holding individuals made a whopping $70-$80,000 a year. We're talking about a two-year program. I ain't mad at that, and you shouldn't be either. Your son or daughter should consider all career opportunities, especially if they find one that offers more job security.

Traditional Four-Year Programs

You have a few types of parents. You have the parents who *just* want their kids to go to school. They may not know much about college, because they didn't go, but they have been told that education provides better opportunities. Then you have the parents who graduated from college and desire for their children to get the experiences they had: pledge a sorority/fraternity, live on their own, enjoy campus life, and experience all that college has to offer. Now, of course, you have the parents who impede on every aspect of their child's life. They coerce their son or daughter to select a major that *they* want them to study and dictate every aspect of the kid's college experience.

This is just a small example of the several styles of parental support out there. You may not relate to any of this. However, if I could give you any advice, this is what I would suggest you do for your child *before* they choose to attend a four-year university.

1.   Push your child to take courses in high school that will prepare them for college rigor. Yes, that means you must do more than wait

for the report card to come home. Pay attention to what they are studying. Keep an open line of communication with their guidance counselor and teachers. Know how they are doing and make sure you enroll them in supplemental instructional programs.

2.   Take advantage of your community college. The college I worked at offered a free course to high school seniors. If your child successfully passes his or her free class, he or she has already earned at least three college credits.

3.   Have you ever heard of advanced placement (AP) courses? You need to ask about them, preferably before your child enrolls in high school. AP courses can turn into college credits. I recently worked at a university where one incoming freshman transferred in over 40 hours of AP credit! That's more than a years' worth of college credit!!!

4.   Once your children begin to prepare to enter college, help them learn the truth about their major. Let's stop letting our kids haphazardly choose majors that won't transition into paid work upon graduation. Study the career outlook for the degree programs in which they are interested.

5.   Last but certainly not least, stop sending your kids to schools that cost an arm, a leg, your house, your retirement, and then the kid is still left with student loans. You must ask yourself *is it worth it?* If your child has a scholarship that will offset the financial burden, that's a different situation. Go for it! I can't tell you where to send your child but have a serious conversation and discuss if it's worth the financial burden. You can get a degree in communications from anywhere…just saying.

Entrepreneurship

We must do a better job educating our kids on the definition of success. Some of us only tell our kids to get a job. We should start preparing them to create their own jobs. The beautiful thing about what we have discussed so far is that if your kids learn to play the game, they can work for themselves or start a side hustle. If they have their own plumbing business, they wouldn't fight over the corner office. If they study speech and language pathology instead of philosophy, they could open their own practice. Or maybe, just maybe, they learn to write their own business plan in high school and decide to use some of their college savings to start that business. We must learn how to think outside of the box. Our kids shouldn't make the same mistakes we made.

It's not that I don't want my son to go to college. I want him to do what works for him. Right now, he loves to build Legos, he's creative, and he appreciates nature. My husband and I do our best to nurture all his interests. Perhaps he will become an engineer. He may have a passion for the hospitality industry. He may find carpentry fulfilling.

He's too young to know now. However, we won't be devastated if chooses not to go away to college and stomp the yard. We are **more** concerned with his ability to thrive throughout his lifetime and build enough economic capital to pass down generational wealth than his temporary experience on someone's campus.

I say all of that to say, let's do better with preparing our kids for post-secondary education. College is fun, but we shouldn't spend the rest of our lives paying for it. There is nothing wrong with pursuing a trade. In fact, it's a probably a better idea for many of our kids. Nevertheless, we cannot keep sending them to college without a plan. If we don't plan, we are doomed to fail. Keep an open mind and research everything before you let your children

settle for a career path that may or may not benefit them long-term.

"I love my husband to death but don't always like him. Life's experiences will throw all types of curve balls. It'll leave you feeling bruised and broken. I remind myself that I may not like him always, but I do love him"- Melanated Queen, 44 years.

Confession Four

Yes, I Love You. I Just Don't Like You

I confess: marriage is hard! Sharing your life with someone is not easy. The night before I got married, my then fiancé and I sat at a local Applebee's engaged in another heated argument. He asked me, "Are you sure you want to do this tomorrow?" We had spent much of our courtship struggling to find a balance between his dreams and mine, and this night was no different.

My mother used to say that during our teenage years, she loved my brother and I, but she didn't like us. I never knew what that meant until I got married. After nearly ten years of marriage, I know exactly what she means. You can love someone to pieces, but there are times when you don't see eye to eye, and you struggle to be cordial with one another. This is a fact. You have good years, bad ones, sometimes really bad ones, but they should never outweigh the good years. The good years should always shine above all. One of the respondents to the confessions survey was a

44-year-old mother of three who spoke to her struggles within her marriage. She stated, "Staying 'in like' with my husband has been a challenge. In fact, one of my New Year's resolutions was to be kinder to him."

I totally get that! For the average single lady waiting on God to "send" that perfect person, understand that every union is different. Please don't put all your hopes and dreams into a unicorn. It's not real. Don't get me wrong, I am 100% pro marriage! I knew when I was very young that I wanted to be married. I came from a two-parent household; my paternal grandparents fulfilled their vows and remained together until my grandfather passed away. It is my understanding that my paternal great-grandparents honored their union until death. I basically come from a family of long-lasting marriages; however, I guarantee you that none of those couples spent every day, every month, or every year in marital bliss.

I can also recall the day I began to understand unconditional love and sacrifice for your mate. My mother and I had some errands to run one day. I can't remember how old I was, but I was pretty young. My father asked us to pick up two ice cream cones from his favorite hot dog stand. Back then, those cones were huge! We finished our running around, and we returned home. My dad met us at the door, ready for his afternoon treat, only to see the two of us sitting in the car empty handed. My mom forgot to get the ice cream. You should have seen his face! He was so disappointed. My mother put the car back in drive, and we headed back out to get the ice cream. Now, I knew she was tired and ready to go in the house. Instead of disappointing my father, she pulled right back out of the driveway, and we picked up his ice cream. I remember thinking at that young tender age, "She must really love him." Yep, she did.

Now that I am a wife and mother, I know what it's like to do stuff you don't feel like doing, but you do it simply because you love that person. Relationships require constant nurturing, compromise, and patience.

Like Forrest Said, You Never Know What You're Gonna Get

I recently had a conversation with a friend of mine. I shared with her the frustration I have with women who judge other women's behavior in THEIR relationships. For my married ladies, how often do you hear your single girlfriend tell you about all the things she would do if she had a husband? It's always that one chick who plans to do cartwheels and acrobats in the bedroom, make the dopest meals, keep her hair and nails done, smell good, smile all the time, laugh at all his jokes, and on and on and on. Meanwhile, you're just smiling and nodding your head, knowing she has no idea what she would do if or when she gets married.

It's easy to imagine the life you want, but living it is another story. When I hear the "when I'm a wife" stories, I never hear about their vision for life with children. You definitely don't hear about their plans for future debt, future disagreements on child rearing, or the classic struggles of finding time to spend with each other.

I was pleased to hear from a 33-year-old melanated Queen who stated, "No marriage is perfect. You will have high and low days. Many days of arguments, like money, kids, and bills. Sex may be fun for the first couple of years you guys are together; the passion is still there and the sexiness. However, do NOT think when you are married you be hittin' every night, nope! Children kind of put that spark on hold."

She's absolutely right! It's difficult to wrap your head around this when you have been waiting for your Boaz for years. I get it. For married ladies, know that you are not alone. Over 60 women responded to my call for action to provide feedback on marriage and family. These ladies didn't hold back. And neither will I. However, it's not just all on the man to make it work. It takes two.

I'll be honest. One of the reasons I believe God allowed me to lose the job I referenced earlier was because I loved my work so much, and I often put my relationships at work before my family at home. Work became my refuge when home life was difficult, and that's not good.

Sometimes it's not just about balancing work, spouse, and children. A 34-year-old melanated Queen with no children shared that the biggest challenge in her marriage was, "Making time for my spouse. Growing together with my mate spiritually and emotionally and connecting with your mate intimately."

Sometimes it's hard to like a person that you love. Though society celebrates independent women, feminism, and "doing bad all by myself", I don't believe that strength lies in independence, it is hanging in there with someone who has made mistakes. Strength is in forgiveness. Strength is in taking your educated hat off and letting him "take care of it".

Children

"Attempting to keep the same fire in my marriage I had when my husband and I first started dating. Sex and

romantic time tend to be on the back burner without realizing it until the petty arguments begin." - Melanated Queen-45 years.

Let's talk about life after you have children. When you are dating a person, you dream about your future, but much of that is tested when your children arrive. A 40-year-old melanated Queen stated that her biggest challenge was communication with her husband.

"We have two totally different styles and beliefs when it comes to raising our children. We had to learn when they were young that the negative stuff that goes on between us does not need to be played out in front of the children. If we disagree about something we talk about it behind closed doors. We need them only to see us loving each other not the other."

It's important to remember that while you and your husband have gotten to know each other, you don't know the personalities of your future children and the dynamic shift that may take place while you attempt to co-parent them. For example, one of the areas I struggled with was martial conflict. I never saw my parents have a disagreement. Therefore, when I had arguments with my husband, I thought it was abnormal. I never witnessed anyone settle a disagreement, so I was traumatized by the entire experience. Eventually, we figured out what works for us, but it was a process. Conflict in front of children is not cool. They shouldn't see you fight but having a calm and respectful disagreement is fine. If it is respectful, it doesn't scare the child, and there is room for a closing resolution.

Again, marriage is tough. Motherhood is though. Therefore, ladies, I know you all are planning to install stripper poles in your future bedrooms, and that's awesome! However, try not to judge that mom who looks jacked up when she's dropping her kids off at school. You never know what that Sista' is going through.

Live Your Life!

Single Queens, I haven't forgotten about you. Times are changing, and the days of living a cookie-cutter lifestyle are long gone. Women are no longer expected to marry straight out of high school, have a house full of babies, and spend the rest of her days only caring for her family. Modern women are educated, career-oriented, and are not accepting any foolishness from the opposite sex. According to the single women who participated in my study, finding a compatible mate is difficult. Most women identified education, finance, and lack of ambition within the dating pool as common barriers to contemporary dating. According to one 35-year-old Queen:

"I don't think many women outside of our culture understand the struggles that black women have as typically being the more educated mate in the relationship. This may mean that a career woman may date someone who financially is unequal and deal with the struggle of the woman being the financial provider. Also, the limited pool of emotionally available single Black men continues to lessen. Black women who are interested in dating Black men are struggling to find Black men who are as established as other men in various races."

It is more common now than ever to marry and start a family later in life. Some women are comfortable with that; others are not. One thing for certain is that men are encouraged to take their time and find that right one. Meanwhile, women are nervously tracking their biological clock. By the time a woman reaches her thirties, her mother, grandmother, aunts, and the entire 11:00 a.m. service at the church is asking when she plans to have babies.

One single Queen spoke to this issue stating, "I feel that people get judged if they are not married by a certain age, but people should know it is ok to be single. Marriage does not justify you as a person." Marriage certainly does not validate you as a person, and I think women need to get over the idea of someone else *completing* them. Nobody can complete you. Nobody! If you show up to your wedding day half a person, then there is something terribly wrong. Figure out what makes you happy as an individual. Naturally, the right person will become drawn to you, and the two of you will *complement* each other.

The only thing I regret is not traveling more when I was single. I was always waiting on someone else to go with me. I was too afraid to venture out alone. For all the single Queens, take this time to do what you love now. This is the only time that your life fully belongs to you. Although you are single, some of you have children, so you understand what I'm talking about. Sharing your life is difficult, and sometimes you may not even like your significant other. Also, if you are like my mother, there are moments when you don't even like your kids. Hence, take a break when you can and enjoy life.

When Things Don't Work Out

Of course, there is divorce. Don't think it hasn't crossed my mind. My husband and I both considered it. I told you it's not always easy. Most days are great, but when it's bad, it's bad. I asked women what is the hardest part about being married. A divorced queen and mother of three shared the following:

"When I was married...it was having to compete with my husband [and] with my kid. [My] husband wanting to go half on bills, but I had to take off when the kid was sick. I was responsible for everything for the kid. I wanted to quit my job because I felt he didn't appreciate my work, then he half way stepped up. [I was] dealing with a selfish man. If he wanted to go out, he just could. He didn't ask if I wanted to do anything or if I wanted to go. But when I made plans with friends, I had to make plans for the kid because he wasn't gonna' watch the baby while I went out."

Living with someone who is not operating as an equal partner is very difficult. It can weigh on a woman's sanity. For some women, their love for their children outweighs their happiness. A 40-year-old queen commented that, "The biggest challenge I face is putting on a happy face for my children by staying in a marriage that I don't want to be in, so that they can grow up with both parents in the same house." Divorce is hard on families. Some women are willing to sacrifice their own happiness for their children. Some are not. Either way, the decision is rarely easy to make, and I respect those Queens who do their best and let God take care of the rest.

For the rest of the Queens out there, just remember that God created marriage. He made Eve for Adam. Through it all, I think that in this day and age, it is still best to choose love. In a marriage, you build together, but you also fail together. You have to take the good with the bad.

But always, always, take time out for you.

"My biggest challenge is keeping my sanity...literally."

Melanated Queen, 44 years old.

Confession Five

Sometimes YouTube Is My Babysitter

I confess: I love being my son's mom. Just to be clear, I love being HIS mom. However, I learned shortly after having my son that I can't be a mom to more than one child and still function as normal person. I confess that though I love being his mom, I don't want to be *a* mom. I know that sounds crazy, but you have some women who are just great at motherhood. They are *bonified* moms. I find the entire experience extremely stressful. Therefore, I prefer to keep it manageable and stick with my one.

A melanated female leader once told me that *Mom* is the most important title I will ever have. I would like to add that it is the *hardest* job I've ever had. Therefore, this chapter is really about the stresses of parenting. And yes, when my kid is enjoying those YouTube videos of other kids playing with toys, or other kids playing video games, sometimes that is my only moment of peace.

When I surveyed melanated women, most of the mothers expressed concern over the lack of time made available to be adequately attentive to their children. Single mothers, such as a 36-year-old mother of one child stated, "I'm a single parent, so my biggest challenges are having enough time and energy to give my child." Modern mothers are responsible for serving as the child's first teacher, making informed decisions regarding the child's formal education, nurturing, financially contributing to the child's welfare, disciplining, listening, and if she is married, fulfilling her duties as a wife as well. It's tough and is one of the many reasons why millennials are choosing to have less children.

When my son started kindergarten, I began a morning ritual with him. First, we pray together. We pray for our family members safe return home each day. After I drop him off at school, I personally pray over him. I ask God to bless him with the spirit of ambition, excellence, wisdom, and the spirit of God. I pray for his health, safety, and happiness. Still, sometimes I get tired. I don't understand how mothers with two or more children do it. When children are little, they require so much of your time and energy. I must admit I was ecstatic when my son was old enough to spend hours alone in his room building Legos. Periodically, I would check on him and ask how his projects are going then return to my Netflix binge.

Mommy guilt is real. Although I strive to be a great mom, I sometimes find myself slipping, and I feel awful about it. When my son was a toddler, I read to him every night. Somehow, and for just a little while, I let that good habit slip away. I suppose it was when he learned to read. He was showing great progress at school, so I let my guard down. I set a goal every Friday to read with him every day over the weekend. Sometimes I look up, and it's Sunday, and the only thing we accomplished was my completion of two seasons of a Netflix original series and hours of him watching YouTube videos of grown folks filming themselves play video games. That's when I feel awful and promise myself that next weekend we will do better. We will go to the library…. or something like that.

The reality is that sometimes all I want to do is lock myself in for the weekend and do much of nothing. I even thought about sending my son to his grandparents' house for the weekend and renting a hotel room. I just want to sleep, eat, and watch TV without feeling bad about doing the same thing at home. When I think of the balancing act that many mothers do each day, I try not to be so hard on myself. For instance, when I asked women to share their challenges raising children, many of them expressed specific values that they try to instill in their kids. A 31-year-old mother of two said her challenge is, "Trying to make sure that I raise two Christian, educated children that are confident in themselves. I try to teach them lessons about violence, bullying, etc."

For many mothers, including myself, keeping up with homework is just a fraction of what we are responsible for monitoring. Explaining to your eight-year-old child why the media reports shootings in Chicago every day becomes part of your regular routine. Having difficult conversations is part of the child rearing. If you're like me, you would prefer to ignore the many questions starting with "why" and "how come" and pretend like everything is just fine, but it's not. Children know it's not, and they look to you to be honest. That's just part of the job.

For working mothers who are struggling to make ends meet, sacrifices are often made just ensure quality time is spent with your kids. One mother, 45, expressed that her struggle was, "Trying to make it financially without working too much overtime that takes me away from my kids." The reality is the role of a parent is just very difficult, especially in today's society. The cost of living has consistently increased over the last few decades, and parents are working more than one job, maintaining a side hustle, and robbing Peter to pay Paul to provide for their families. A 33-year-old melanated Queen affirmed that her biggest challenge is balancing all the barriers of parenting such as "living off paycheck to paycheck, trying to keep food on table, ensuring that they are doing what they are supposed to be doing, making sure they have clothes to wear and a roof over their heads."

Unless you come from generational wealth, it is extremely hard to manage these days. Therefore, parents have the responsibility to meet their children's basic needs with little available resources. I am blessed to have a husband who serves as a partner in parenting. When I'm tired, our son can hang out with dad for a few hours. In the beginning, most of the responsibility fell on me. As my son grew older, his dad became his playmate and best friend. However, in order to make ends meet, he has to work as much as he can to provide for us, so he's not always home. Trust me, I have no complaints about it. However, there are so many mothers out there who bear the responsibility of raising a child alone. One Queen, age 39 and mother of sons, shared that her children have different fathers, and she is constantly worried about money. She suffers from lack of sleep and often finds herself drained from it all. As a result, she frequently experiences a lack of motivation and finds it difficult to strive to reach her full potential.

Today's culture celebrates the liberation of women, feminism, independence, and the "I can do bad all my myself" mindset. However, some melanated moms are transparent about the challenges of raising a child(ren) alone. One 36-year-old melanated queen stated, "Since I am a single parent, the biggest challenge is trying to compensate for the absence of the father. There are many lessons that I will be unable to teach. Lastly, having a very limited support system is a huge challenge. It truly does take a village." Although Black women have proven throughout history that we can do a lot with very little, it is still very difficult to be the best mom you can be all by yourself. Indeed, it takes a village.

For those Sista's making it happen on your own, know that you are never really alone. God is with you always. Even when we don't have a spouse, a significant other, a best friend, or a parent to help, God has blessed us all with instincts. I admire how my husband overcame a tough childhood with little positive direction and reinforcement and still grew up to be a stable, loving, and supportive husband and father. His instincts kicked in and he chose to use them.

A similar experience was shared by a brave mom who said, "My biggest challenge being a mother is trying to overcome my childhood issues and raise my children how I would have desired to be. I had a very distant and unconnected relationship with my mother growing up, and I'm determined to set a platform of high standards and plenty of love with my children." Yes, Queen! You must break the cycle, and I love to see melanated people change the trajectory of their lineage. We have the power to do that, and it's time we learn that God has given us the tools. We just need to recognize *when* there is a problem that needs to be fixed.

Consequently, I realize that I am doing the best that I can with my son. Yeah, sometimes we skip reading on Friday nights, and he spends a little too much time on the computer tablet, but I have to give us all a break sometimes. The important thing is that we recognize when enough is enough, and we make a concerted effort to improve our child's learning and social climate. You shouldn't

be so hard on yourself either. You are doing your best; now let God

guide you through the rest.

"Black women are not viewed as pretty unless they are a certain complexion, body type, and hair."-Melanated Queen, 38 years.

Confession Six

Colorism: Stop it!

I confess: my Black is beautiful. Your Black is beautiful. Melanin is beautiful.

My biggest issue with the Black community is colorism. I truly believe that if we learn to love ourselves and appreciate our authentic beauty, we can conquer the ideology that was placed on our hearts and souls centuries ago.

I remember watching music videos when I was a little girl. All of the women had fair skin, long hair, and they were always portrayed as the love interest of the artist. I knew early on that there was a preference for lighter skinned Black women. There wasn't anything I could do about my skin, but I always wanted long hair. Like many other melanated girls, when my mother braided my hair at night, she made me put a stocking cap on. Well, I didn't want to cut the legs out of my stocking cap. I wanted to keep them on so that I can have a long, brown ponytail. My other favorite hair-do was a t-shirt. Yes, a t-shirt. This style was created by wearing the opening of the head over and around my forehead area. This gave me the look I was going for, long and flowing hair around my face and down my back.

Looking back on it, I understand now that many of those women I idealized in those videos wore weaves. However, many of them did not. The music industry made a conscience effort to seek out mixed-race women to fulfill the role of the leading lady in their videos. Fortunately, I was blessed to have parents who frequently told me I was pretty. We had discussions in our house regarding skin tone, and my parents always spoke proudly of both their fathers, who had deep, dark black skin. However, for many darker skinned girls with short curly hair, they are left to discover their beauty on their own…if they ever do.

The problem is this: many melanated people pass this ideology down to their children. My heart hurts for those children who do not have adults in their lives to tell them they are beautiful. This vicious cycle of self-hatred continues to manifest with each generation and it's pretty sickening. When my son was born, I grew very tired and angry over the so-called compliments he received on his complexion. Grown people were telling me that my son was "a perfect brown". And oh Lord, don't let him play in the sun for a few hours. I showed a woman a picture of him one summer, and she asked, "What happened to his beautiful honey skin?" What?!?!? Are you serious?!?!? So, what if he was naturally darker? Would he still receive compliments?

There are women who deliberately seek out men with lighter complexions, just so they can give birth to lighter skinned babies. Stop it! Love who you love. I'm not knocking people who date or marry lighter complexion Blacks. This is no shade or disrespect to our light skinned brothers and sisters. My issue is not with them; my issue is with melanated people who honor light over dark. I take issue with parents who make derogatory remarks against dark skinned black people, especially in front of their children. Stop it! I take issue with people who approach light skinned children and tell them how cute they are and say little to empower the darker skinned child standing right next to them.

There is no such thing as *good* hair. Our hair is beautiful, no matter the texture. Stop it! My long stocking cap and t-shirt hair didn't last long. Thankfully, my parents only bought me dolls that looked like me. My entire doll collection was Black and beautiful. Therefore, it was so much easier for me to understand that the images I saw on T.V. were not a true reflection of Black pride.

Stop obsessing over non-melanated people. Stop calling dark skinned people ugly. Stop using the word ugly against melanated people period. Your children are watching and listening. If you call a melanated person a derogatory name, how do think your children will internalize that? Stop it!

The brown paper bag test was real. It is sad that the tactic is still used, just not with an actual bag. As a people, we still struggle to see our own beauty.

Tell your son or daughter they are beautiful. Tell them that they are God's chosen people. Share with them that their skin has been kissed by sun which brings forth light and life. Stop the self-hate. Start loving yourselves.

Confession Seven

Jesus Is My Savior. That's My Story, and I'm Sticking to It

I confess: I don't like going to church, at least not traditional church. When I say traditional church, I mean the kind of church where you can't walk down the center of the aisle, the pastor asks for last year's tax return to determine your tithes, and the praise team performs longer than the sermon is delivered.

I just can't do it. I grew up in a small, store front church setting. We didn't even call it church, we called it Bible class. There were not many rules, you gave what you could, and our pastor did not receive a salary. I know, shocking right? A pastor who did not collect a salary. He had something called a *pension.* He worked all his life (can you hear the sarcasm?) He taught the word for free because the word was given to him for free. We all get it for free, but I digress.

I struggle with the idea that the Black community has a church on every street corner, which circulates much of the Black dollar, and we still don't have institutions that improve the climate of our own communities. Instead of working together to build resources with the money that the Black working class continuously pours into the church, pastors, deacon boards, and other church leaders, continue to work in silos. They rarely partner with one another. There is an increased level of narcissism among leaders, and members are left with a false sense of community that does very little to change their cycle of poverty.

My intent is not to bash the church, but I challenge church members to take some time to truly reflect on what the *church* has done as an institution to improve your livelihood. Black people love to hear a good sermon. We get excited when a leader stands before us and tells us everything is going to be alright. We love a good speech. We are moved by words. We are enlightened by charisma. We get excited when the pastor uses slang or secular innuendos in his or her sermon because it makes us feel like he or she "gets it". We get pumped up by promises, and we pay our tithes without hesitation because we feel so good at the end of a theatric service.

I know I'm rubbing some of you the wrong way, but let's face it. There is no other Black financial institution stronger than the

Black church. Unfortunately, there seems to be a stronger interest in providing a comfortable life for your pastor and first lady than there is for securing small business loans for members and purchasing franchises so that the young people in the congregation have jobs. There appears to be an unnatural obsession for pastors, first ladies, and other so-called church leaders. There seems to be an unwritten school of thought within the Black church that God speaks through pastors more than He speaks directly to you. I see social media posts like this every day. Folks will post a pastor's sermon regarding something that resonated with them. The caption almost always reads, "This is my confirmation". My question is why? Clearly you have been talking to God about this issue, or perhaps you opted not to share your thoughts with God. However, you have been feeling some kind of way about it for some time, yet, the minute pastor so and so addresses the issue, BOOM! You now have confirmation. Something is wrong there.

I accepted Jesus as my Lord and Savior at a very young age. I have always had a direct line of communication with God. Don't misunderstand me; I believe that God will and can use others to speak to you. It is my experience that this happens when I don't hear his voice, or when I choose to ignore His voice. God speaks to me subtlety. He speaks to me through small whispers. Some people call it instincts. Sometimes you just know something, and if you are a believer, you know that it's HIM who orders our steps. Nonetheless, you have to let him speak to you. Some of us melanated folks are letting our so called spiritual leaders direct our paths. Let's not forget that they are human too. They make mistakes just like we do. This is why I question the obsession over pastoral leaders.

In my humble opinion, pastors are teachers. That's it and that's all. They teach the Word of God, or at least they should. I can't begin to count how many churches I have visited that not once opened the Bible and taught a lesson directly from the Word. Instead, I was entertained by yet another feel-good speech.

I say all of this to say: I love God with all my heart and soul. Let me be clear, Jesus is God. I follow Jesus. I know that Jesus died for my sins. I have faith that his Word is true. It is because of his love for me that I do not feel inclined to allow any person, man or woman to intercede in our relationship.

Now, of course, not all churches are as I described. There are some great exceptions. Some of you attend churches that have built schools, businesses, and ministries that empower melanated people to thrive economically. I don't have a problem with congregations that operate with the intent to build and uplift the community. I am happy whenever I hear about the work that's going on in grass-roots movement churches that get in the trenches and serve the people. I support those congregations that feed the homeless, provide a safe haven for those in need, help those who could use help with bills that are overdue, buy school clothes for Sister Jessica's kids, and buy a suit for Mr. Johnson because he can't afford one for his job interview. I applaud those ministries, and I believe that God continues to grant favor over them.

I have a problem with people who worship their pastors instead of God. I have a problem with pastors who live a life of luxury off the offerings of members but do little to construct institutions that help lift them out of poverty. I have a problem with pastors getting paid to teach God's *free* word. I have a problem with women who focus more on their desire to be a pastor's first lady than lady of God. I have a problem with the hypnosis that melanated people are under as it relates the power of church leaders. If you are not changing the life opportunities of melanated people, you have no power. You are merely a figure head. A show. An entertainer. And in many cases, a thief and a liar.

On a lighter note, there is something that makes me laugh but gets on my last nerve. I get so irritated when the pastor asks the congregation to turn to your neighbor and say this and that. It's always, "Turn to your neighbor and say, 'neighbor, I don't know about you, but God has blessed me," I. Can't. Stand. That (with the clap in-between words)! I'm not saying it's a terrible thing. I just have to confess that I absolutely hate when I'm asked to participate in church. I don't want to turn to my neighbor and say anything. I want to get back to our conversation on Shadrach, Meshach, and Abednego. But again, I digress.

God is everywhere and for everyone. No church, religion, practice, or belief can change the fact that there is only one and true living God. This topic is so important to me because I believe that if we, as melanated people, stop letting our ego stand in our way, we can be the true servant leaders that God has called us to be. Servant leadership is all about putting the needs of others before ourselves.

Some of your pastors are doing the exact opposite. Start holding your church accountable. Make the same demands on Sunday that you make Monday through Friday. Make the same demands of your pastors as you do for your fellow melanated Brothers and Sisters who are in the daily trenches with you.

To that end, Jesus is my one and only savior. That's my story, and I'm sticking to it.

"My challenges are raising young men. In our neighborhood, they see quick money, and they want it too, especially when their friends are getting it."- Melanated Queen 51-years

Confession Eight

I Can't Be Calm, I'm Raising a Black Son

I always assumed that I would have a daughter. I suppose I imagined my life as a mother mirroring the relationship my mother and I have. My biggest worry would be centered on keeping her away from teenage pregnancy, drugs, school fights, and abusive relationships. I just never thought that I would have a son.

Then, as I planned my pregnancy, I came to the realization that I would have a baby boy. On May of 2009, my five-month check-up confirmed that I was going to be raising a Black son. When my husband and I decided to plan for our child, I began to pray for blessings to be bestowed on our future baby. I prayed that God blessed him with good health. I didn't pray for just physical health; I prayed for his holistic well-being. I prayed that God blessed him with physical, mental, emotional, spiritual, and social health. I had it all planned out. I wanted him to learn Spanish by age three. I debated over private versus public education, and we definitely were going to visit the library once a week because literacy is the path to freedom. I had so many plans for him. I obsessed over education because I worked in higher education, and I saw the good, the bad, and the ugly behind the college preparation process. I wanted my child to be ready.

Before he was even born, I had a plan ready and prepared. The problem is I never thought about the experience he would truly have outside of our home and the love his father and I would give him. I only saw him as our baby and not the Black boy that he was. By age three, he didn't learn Spanish; he actually struggled to communicate period. I had him evaluated for speech, and he started therapy. That's when we really began to see what raising a Black boy in America is really like.

When I asked other melanated Queens what challenges they faced raising children, one 36-year-old mother shared that she tries to "Keep them structured, being a role model, teaching boys how to be respectable men, making time for everyone, paying for activities, and making sure their immediate needs are met." African American boys are born with a target on their back. The majority of the youth killed by gun violence are Black boys, though the numbers for our girls are drastically increasing as well. As a mother, I find myself challenged with the task of balancing my emotions and logic as it relates to advocating for my son. Let me explain.

I'm often reminded of two young Black men who should have lived long happy lives and died as old men. However, they didn't have the opportunity to grow old. At age 14, they were both murdered by the hands of white supremacists. Historically, it was common to torture, beat, and violently murder Black males for sport. However, the two stories that stand out most to me were the murders of Emmett Till and George Stinney Jr.

If you don't know their stories, research it. Let it sink in. Both boys were only 14 years of age when they were killed. Both boys were killed because of an accusation related to white females. Both were innocent. Emmett was a child who shouldn't have lost his life for allegedly whistling at a white woman. It was impossible for little George, who was 95 pounds, to kill two white girls. George couldn't read, yet he allegedly signed a confession. Again, research their stories. Don't forget them. Don't forget any of the Black souls who lost their lives to white supremacy. I'm sure when those boys were born, the last thing their mothers wanted to think about was the possibility that within in a few short years, those children would be tortured, and in George's case, executed in an electric chair.

Fast forward to 2018; the school to prison pipeline, gang violence, school suspension and expulsion, miseducation, misdiagnosis of special education, murder by the hands of law enforcement, having the wrong complexion for protection, and the removal of fathers in the Black home have all served as systematic forms of modern lynching. The women who participated in my survey shared their struggles with raising sons. One 33-year-old mother shared her struggles stating that they consisted of "raising and preparing young Black kids in today's society along with finding good schools, and neighborhoods." Her statement speaks directly to my concerns expressed earlier. Black boys are held at the bottom of the totem pole, and they remain there most, if not all, of their lives.

Too many mothers are still grieving the loss of their sons due to the violent climate of their neighborhoods. Other mothers have lost their sons to the prison industrial complex, in which the grooming process starts in the elementary schools. Raising a Black boy in America is hard. Many participating mothers shared that they grapple with raising their boys in a racist environment, and they often do it alone.

"Not having the support of his Black father and the school system (we live in a predominately white area) not seeing his dark skin as a threat. Not being able to find an affordable area to live that has a great mix of nationalities without the violence and poverty"
Melanated Queen, 39 years.

As I mentioned earlier, we had everything planned out for our son. It was rough in the beginning. The moment we realized he suffered from a delay in speech, we began to experience the process of labeling Black boys in the school system. We experienced a school social worker attempt to discredit his ability to learn at age three. We began to understand how desperate other Black families are for a quality education, when we began to pay for private school. After three and a half years in a private, "Christian" environment, we finally realized that money doesn't buy everything. They miseducate Black boys in private schools too.

We decided to take matters into our own hands. During the process of completing my dissertation, I learned that statistically, Black boys who have been taught to value their heritage perform better in school. We make a conscious effort to discuss sensitive topics in his presence, so that he understands where we stand on the issue. We hold him accountable for what he learns at school. The rule in our home is that our son is required to tell us what he learned every day. This process promotes open communication and builds a level of trust, so that he understands that we care and are deeply invested in his life outside of our home. It also shows him that we mean business.

We remind our son that he is smart, and that our expectation is for him to excel. We invest in toys like Legos, so that he can practice building and exercising his creativity. We bring him into our conversations because we don't believe in the old saying children should be seen, not heard. Children have a voice. If you silence them now, they will be conditioned to believe that they will never have a voice.

Now, I realize that I used the word *we* frequently in the last paragraph. I'm married, and my husband is heavily involved in our son's life. However, this is not the case for many Black mothers.

"I am a single mother of a son with no participation from his father. There is no financial, physical, or emotional support from the other parent." Melanated Queen, 35 years old.

There are a lot of single mothers out there who are struggling to manage the great responsibility of raising a Black boy alone. Women are charged with providing, supporting, listening, and protecting Black sons without the emotional and financial support of a partner. I can recall how emotional I was when I first received a call from my son's school regarding his performance. It took the encouragement from the two most important men in his life, his father and grandfather, to keep me grounded. No matter how educated I was and how much experience I had, nothing could prepare me for facing someone who sought to find error in my child.

That's why we all need a support system. Find a close relative, friend, pastor, or tutor that you can **trust** who will be there for you when it's time to go to parent-teacher conference or IEP meetings. Now, the key word is *trust*. Too many children are dying by the hands of their mother's boyfriends. Everybody doesn't need to be in your child's life. If you are single and trying to raise a Black boy, this is not the time to be "bad and boujee". It's time to prepare your son for this thing called life. His White counterparts will have a support system out there to defend them if they commit senseless crimes against your son. Look at George Zimmerman and Darren Wilson. They became millionaires after killing our sons. When your son is out there, he won't have that kind of aid. Thus, this is not the time to be independent and proud. Find a good support system and prepare your Black boy.

When I think of Emmett, George, Trayvon, Michael, Tamir, Laquan, and the countless other young Black souls taken from their mothers' arms far too soon, I am reminded that it's never over. I've been guilty of letting my guard down but never again. We must do our best to protect them when they are young and prepare them for when they grow older.

"My biggest challenges are knowing when to let go and allow them to make their own mistakes to learn from, teaching them to be leaders and not followers, and instilling in them that they can grow up to be whatever they want, but also knowing that the world will put up every barrier possible to deter them." Melanated Queen, 40 years old.

This Queen said it best. For Black boys, the barriers are deep and may feel impossible to overcome. But as she said, it is our job to instill in them that they can be whatever they want. That's a fact.

"I believe a lot of challenges experienced by black women also stem from not having a better support system from other black women or black people in general. Stemming from slavery, Africans were treated differently because of their skin color even today this practice still exists. Because of this practice, our people have been so divided, and we still are. In corporate America, Caucasians will help each other out; therefore, you will see their friends and family members get the promotions and get the better paying jobs, the same with Asians and Hispanics, but African Americans are hesitant to help each other succeed and excel because we see our own people as a threat. This one aspect has continued to keep African Americans down and until we realize that we have more power than what the media or society portrays, this cycle will continue in our people". Melanated Queen, 36 years old.

Confession Nine

Melanated Queens Shouldn't Wear Pink Knitted Hats

Have you ever seen the movie Claudine? It was released in the early 1970's and it starred Diahann Carroll and James Earl Jones. Diahann Carroll played the role of Claudine, a 36-year-old single mother of 6. She was also on welfare. There is a scene in the movie where the social worker is spotted coming down the street. The kids make an announcement that the social worker was coming. Everyone had their role. They hid items that looked new or expensive. They rolled up the carpet. They pretty much arranged the home to look as poor as possible.

I asked my mom what that was about, and she told me that the movie was very accurate. Social workers in those days were paid to ensure you had nothing. You couldn't work, and you better not have a man in the house or you risked losing all your benefits.

What I don't understand is why melanated queens don't see or understand that this was the strategic plan to remove Black men out of their homes. Now, we have normalized independence and shunned Black men for not having the education and career paths that we have.

Ok, so now that I have set the stage, let's fast forward to 2018. I can't help but to notice that melanated people have the tendency to get caught up in the hype of feel good speeches at awards shows, hashtags, social media challenges, and other BS social movements that do very little to change the climate of Black people in America. I find it even more disturbing that Black women are invited to march with the feminist and throw a hashtag on our social media post to bring awareness to what is allegedly going on in Hollywood, but when it comes down to addressing issues that truly impact **our** community, there is silence from the other side.

Now let me be clear on who I am talking about. I'm talking about the feminist. I am **not** moved by their speeches, and their hashtags are nothing more than a strategy to make moves that benefit *them*. But, I have an idea. Let's throw *#MeToo* and *#TimesUp* on some real issue that impact melanated people. *#TimesUp* on the miseducation of African American children in the American public and private school systems. *#MeToo* While you march to prove you are equal to the man you go home to, Black women have been systematically separated from their men on an emotional, economic, and physical level for hundreds of years. *#TimesUp* on the mass incarceration of Black men, women, and children. *#TimesUp* on the fear that Black people live with every day. *#TimesUp* on the school to prison pipeline for Black children. *#MeToo* on the daily struggles of sharing your life with a Black man who has created a contingency plan for his family in the event that his life is cut short after an interaction with police. *#TimesUp* on the defamation of Black marriages, Black families, and Black love. *#MeToo* for Sandra Bland and the many other Black women who have been killed due to White supremacy.

Where is the Women's March and *#MeToo* when Black women mourn the loss of their children who have been murdered in the streets of America? *#MeToo* for my childhood memory of listening to my parents coach my older brother on how to interact with the police when or if he is pulled over. *#TimesUp* on forgetting that despite what's going on in Hollywood, Black men are at the bottom of the totem pole in education, employment, and fair treatment. *#TimesUp* on the misdiagnosis of ADHD and any other disability that lands Black boys in unwarranted special education.

Years ago, as a sociology major, I told my undergraduate feminist professor that Black women had no place in the feminist movement. I said it then and I'll say it again. If a social movement does not unite, strengthen, and empower Black women AND men **equally**…miss me with it.

The reality is that Black men have been painted as hyper-sexual animals for centuries. For some of them, they can't seem to stay away from the forbidden fruit, no matter how many of their ancestors were beaten, tortured, and lynched over it. Feminists use their movement to navigate their way to the top of hierarchical chain. Meanwhile, men have been losing their jobs, reputation, and livelihood over unproven allegations.

It's one thing to let this happen to their men. But wait, don't forget I have a Black son, a Black husband, a Black father, and a Black brother. Let's be real about who we are talking about. Do you think I am really going to allow stories that emerge decades later to inspire me to turn my back on Black men such as Russell Simmons, Bill Cosby, and countless others? Should their legacy, their contributions to Black culture, and their name be tarnished because of what a woman *said* happened? Do I need to remind you of Emmett Till and George Stinney Jr.? Who was the common denominator?

When a melanated queen can justify our participation in the feminist movement, I'll take it all back. Until then, they can keep their hashtags and feel good speeches. I stand with Black men, and I rest my case.

Confession Ten

I Just Want a Simple Life

I remember the day I realized I was going to pursue my doctoral degree. It was a Saturday. I was doing what I always do, buying groceries. I sat in the car for a few moments and thought about my routine. My son was much smaller then, so our evenings were pretty much the same. I came home from work, everyone ate dinner, we watched a little T.V., we had bath time, we read a story, and we said good night. Then we hit repeat and did it all again the next day. On Sundays, I visited my parents, even though I saw them most days out of the week, as they help tremendously with our son. Saturdays were different because every other Saturday was grocery day.

The day I decided to pursue my doctorate, I realized that I wanted something more. I wanted to break the monotony and be challenged. I also had an urge to pursue research because this was also during the time that I began to understand the complexities of raising a Black boy. Mostly, I was just bored.

A few months later, I applied and was accepted to my doctoral program. It was only after I graduated that I realized that my boredom was just what I always wanted, a simple life.

I never wanted to be famous. I always wanted to be educated, married, a mother, a homeowner, and happy. I was living the dream and didn't even realize it. Presently, I focus on enjoying those moments. Grocery shopping, paying bills, working, writing, and being an overall adult is exactly what I prayed. If I am doing those things, I know that I am still blessed. Never again will I complain about my monotonous schedule. It brings me peace.

However, I challenge you to think about what life you want. *Why* do you want it? Finally, *what* steps have you taken to live that life? Stop waiting for the imaginary husband to fall out the sky. If you are with someone you love, and he loves you, what are you waiting for? Choose love and be happy. If you want that promotion, ask for it. If you don't get it, create your own opportunity. If you want to be a homeowner, learn as much as you can about credit and budgeting, and buy that home. Take that vacation. Visit that friend. Have fun.

Do I feel strong about the opinions expressed in this book? Absolutely! I think that Black people in America have a lot to proud of. But, no matter what, I can't control everything. I can't change everyone's life with a few words. But I hope to inspire. And I pray for continued happiness and peace. Despite the complexities of the modern Black woman, we have a lot to live for.

Life is short. I choose to live my life as simple as possible. Be sure to live yours as *authentically* as possible.

Peace!

Thank You

First and foremost, thank you to my Lord and Savior Jesus Christ. Far too many melanated people have lost faith in you, but you continue to be faithful. Thank you for blessing me and my family. Thank you for continuously being a light unto my path.

I want to thank my husband, my son, my parents, and all of my friends and family who help contribute to my overall being. I love you all.

Thank you, Helena Fields, for serving as reader and editor of *Confessions of a Melanated Queen*. I appreciate your friendship and support.

Thank you to Carrie Jemii and Diamond McNulty of McNulty International and Intelligent Marketing Principals for designing the book cover and continuously supporting me throughout all my endeavors. And finally, thank you to the women who contributed their stories, quotes, and personal struggles with me. This book is more authentic, relatable, and real because of you.

About the Author

Dr. Lauren Meeks is an advocate for ending social, economic, and educational disparities among underserved populations. With a background in higher education, youth development, and workforce development, Dr. Meeks is committed to following and exhibiting the principles of servant leadership.

Dr. Meeks earned a Bachelor of Arts degree in Sociology, a Master of Arts in Political and Justice Studies, and a Doctor of Education in Ethical Leadership. She is the founder of We City, NFP, and frequently blogs about issues related to marriage and family. Dr. Meeks can be reached at laurentmeeks@gmail.com

Be sure to continue to follow her blog at

www.confessionsofamelanatedqueen.com.